THE WORLD OF PLANTS

HOW DO PLANTS MAKE THEIR OWN FOOD?

by Ruth Owen

PowerKiDS press™

New York

Published in 2015 by The Rosen Publishing Group, Inc.
29 East 21st Street, New York, NY 10010

First Edition

Produced for Rosen by Ruby Tuesday Books Ltd
Editor for Ruby Tuesday Books Ltd: Mark J. Sachner
US Editor: Joshua Shadowens
Designer: Emma Randall

Photo Credits:
Cover, 1, 4–5, 6–7, 8, 9, 10 (bottom), 11, 12–13, 14–15, 17, 20–21, 22–23, 24–25, 26–27, 28 © Shutterstock; 9 (top), 10 (top), 16 © Public Domain; 18–19, 29 © Ruby Tuesday Books.

Publisher's Cataloging Data

Owen, Ruth.
How do plants make their own food? / by Ruth Owen, first edition.
p. cm. — (The world of plants)
Includes index.
ISBN 978-1-4777-7149-5 (library binding) — ISBN 978-1-4777-7150-1 (pbk.) —
ISBN 978-1-4777-7151-8 (6-pack)
1. Plants — Nutrition — Juvenile literature. I. Owen, Ruth, 1967–. II. Title.
QK867.O94 2015
580—d23

Manufactured in the United States of America

CPSIA Compliance Information: Batch #WS14PK8: For Further Information contact Rosen Publishing, New York, New York at 1-800-237-9932

Contents

Making Food with Light

When you need energy, you make a sandwich or eat an apple. Birds busily peck at seeds or pull worms from the soil. Squirrels hunt for acorns, while raccoons check out trash cans for tasty scraps. But what about plants? How do these living things get the energy they need to grow and stay healthy?

Unlike animals, plants can't move around to find or catch food. So plants make their own food inside their leaves using water, **carbon dioxide** gas, and sunlight. This process is called **photosynthesis**.

The word "photosynthesis" comes from the word "photo," which means "light," and the word "synthesis," which means "putting together." Using light, plants put together water and carbon dioxide and make the food they need to survive.

Water for Photosynthesis

Plants use their roots to obtain the water they need to carry out photosynthesis.

The roots of most plants grow underground in soil. Some plants have many roots that spread out in the soil horizontally. Others have one thick main root, called a taproot, that grows vertically down into the ground. Thin, hairlike roots sprout from a plant's thicker main root or roots.

Roots spreading out

Taproot

Hairlike roots

A plant's hairlike roots take in water from the soil. Then the water travels up through the plant's thicker roots into its stem. Here, a system of tubes, called **xylem**, deliver the water throughout the plant's many stems or branches to the leaves, where it can be used for photosynthesis.

Trunk, or
main stem

Roots

Carbon Dioxide for Photosynthesis

In addition to water, plants need carbon dioxide in order for photosynthesis to take place.

Carbon dioxide is a gas that's in the air all around us. When people and other animals exhale during breathing, they breathe out carbon dioxide into the air.

Plants take in carbon dioxide with their leaves. On the underside of a leaf there are tiny pores, or holes, called **stomata**. A single pore is called a stoma. These holes are so tiny they can only be seen with a microscope. Carbon dioxide enters a plant's leaves through the stomata. Then the gas spreads out inside the leaf to where it is needed for photosynthesis.

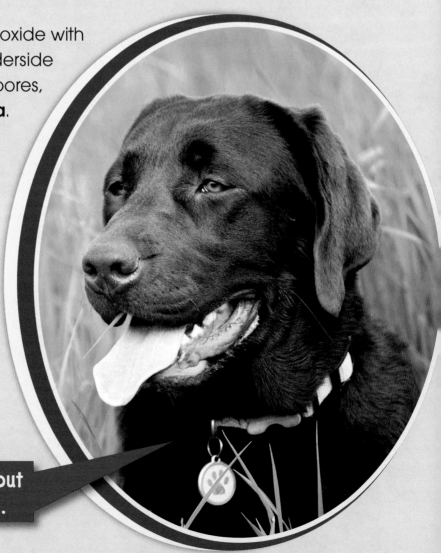

Animals breathe out carbon dioxide.

A stoma on a tomato plant leaf seen through a microscope

Tomato plant leaf

9

Green Food Factories

Inside the cells of a leaf there are structures, or parts, called **chloroplasts**. Photosynthesis takes place in the chloroplasts.

Chloroplasts contain a substance called **chlorophyll**. It's this substance that gives plants their green color.

The chlorophyll in a plant's leaves traps sunlight. Then the chlorophyll uses the light to turn water and carbon dioxide into a type of sugary plant food called glucose. The food made by photosynthesis travels through a plant in a system of tubes called **phloem**. The phloem carry food from the leaves to wherever it is needed inside a plant.

Chloroplasts

Cell wall

Cells in a leaf that have been magnified hundreds of times

The chlorophyll in leaves gives them their green color.

11

Making Food and Oxygen

From grass in a lawn to tall trees in a forest, plants are busy cooking up their own special kind of food all around us.

A plant uses the sugars it makes during photosynthesis for growth and health. The sugars are also converted into a substance called starch that can be stored in leaves, stems, and roots. Plants can use this stored food at times when there is less sunlight around.

During photosynthesis, plants don't only make their food. They also make oxygen. Plants release the oxygen they produce into the air through the stomata in their leaves. Without trees and other plants making oxygen, humans and animals would not be able to breathe!

Transpiration

Plants don't only release oxygen from their leaves. They also release water vapor into the air.

When the stomata on a plant's leaves open to take in carbon dioxide, water inside the leaves evaporates into the air as water vapor. This process of releasing water vapor into the air is called **transpiration**.

Transpiration helps the plant by cooling it, just as sweating helps cool a human's body. Also, as water evaporates from a plant's leaves, it causes more water to be drawn up from the roots, through the xylem, to the leaves. This flow of water through the plant is similar to what happens when a person sucks liquid through a straw. Transpiration ensures that there is a constant supply of water traveling from the plant's roots to its leaves for photosynthesis.

Carbon dioxide ● ● ● ● ● ▶
Water vapor ● ● ● ● ● ● ● ▷
Oxygen ● ● ● ● ● ● ● ● ● ● ▶

Nutrients for Healthy Growth

Plants aren't able to get everything they need for growth and health during photosynthesis.

To grow and remain healthy, people need foods that give them energy. They also need to eat foods that give them extra **nutrients**, such as vitamins and **minerals**. Plants are the same. They need the sugary food they produce during photosynthesis. They also need nutrients such as nitrogen, potassium, calcium, and magnesium. These nutrients can be found dissolved in water in the soil. Most plants take in these nutrients through their roots when they take in water.

A young cabbage plant that needs more nutrients

Without nutrients from the soil, plants may struggle to grow and produce leaves, flowers, fruits, and seeds. They may also have difficulty making the green chlorophyll in their leaves that they need for photosynthesis.

A healthy young cabbage plant that is obtaining enough nutrients from the soil

Resting for the Winter

During the months of winter, it can be hard for plants to make food.

Winter days are short, with fewer hours of sunlight than in spring and summer. In many areas, it rains less in winter, and any water in the soil may freeze.

With little sunlight and water available, a plant's leaves cannot carry out photosynthesis. For this reason, many plants stop growing and rest for winter. Their leaves, flowers, and sometimes stems shrivel and die. Some plants leave only bare stems above ground. It looks as if the plants have died, but their roots are still alive underground.

These garden plants are growing new shoots and leaves in spring.

In spring, as sunlight increases and rain showers fall, the plants push up new shoots from underground. Soon they begin growing new leaves for photosynthesis.

A new shoot uncurling

This fern plant looks like it has died. In spring, however, new shoots start to grow.

Trees in Winter

Like other plants, many trees rest during winter.

With sunlight and water in short supply, a tree's leaves cannot make enough food to feed the large plant. Growing and keeping leaves healthy uses a lot of energy, too. So, in readiness for the tough months of winter, many trees drop their leaves in the fall. The tree's trunk, bare branches, and roots then stop growing and rest until spring to save energy. Trees that drop their leaves in the fall are called **deciduous** trees.

Before a tree's leaves drop, they may turn yellow, orange, or brown. This is because when the leaves stop making food, they also stop making green chlorophyll. As the green color fades, the leaves' other colors, which are normally hidden, start to show through.

A green leaf in summer

A leaf that has stopped making chlorophyll in fall

Woods in the fall

A dead leaf

Making Food All Year Round

Some trees do not drop their leaves in the fall. These trees are called coniferous, or evergreen, trees.

Coniferous trees often live in cold or very dry **habitats** where sunlight and water are in short supply spring, summer, fall, and winter. These trees don't drop all their leaves in the fall, but lose and regrow small quantities of leaves all year long. This strategy means the trees always have leaves, and can make food whenever they get the chance.

Coniferous trees do not grow large, flat leaves, like maple trees or oak trees. Many types grow leaves that look like thin, green needles. Like all leaves, however, these needles are able to use water, carbon dioxide, and sunlight to make food for the trees.

Each of these thin green needles is a leaf.

Coniferous trees growing on a dry, rocky mountainside

The Lungs of the Planet

You may have heard people say that Earth's rain forests are the "lungs" of our planet. That's because the millions of trees and other plants in rain forests produce enormous quantities of oxygen as they photosynthesize.

Rain forest

These forests also remove enormous quantities of carbon dioxide from the air. Removing this gas from Earth's **atmosphere** is more important than ever as human activities are creating too much carbon dioxide. Burning fuel in vehicles or in power plants to make electricity creates carbon dioxide and other harmful gases that collect in Earth's atmosphere. These gases then trap heat on Earth, which is causing **global warming**.

When rain forests are cut down, trees and other plants that are helping remove carbon dioxide from the air are destroyed!

Empty ground that was once home to trees and other plants.

Essential for Survival

Without photosynthesis, plants could not survive. Neither could we!

Humans and other animals need plants for food. People eat the leaves, roots, stems, flowers, fruits, and seeds of many plants. Bread, cookies, cereal, and pasta are made from plants such as wheat and oats. Without grass and other plants to feed animals such as sheep and cattle, we would have no meat, milk, cheese, ice cream, or yogurt.

We all eat foods that come from plants every day.

Plants make the oxygen we need to breathe and remove the carbon dioxide we don't need from the air.

Trees, grass, wildflowers, and other plants don't only make our world look beautiful. They also make our lives on Earth possible!

Investigating the World of Plants

INVESTIGATION 1:

Sunlight for Photosynthesis

In order for photosynthesis to take place a plant needs sunlight. So what happens to a plant if it doesn't get enough light? Find out in this investigation.

Step 1:
Stand each plant in a saucer to catch any water that leaks from the pots. Put one plant inside a dark cupboard. Place the other plant on a sunny windowsill.

Step 2:
Water the plants regularly to keep their soil moist. Make sure that both plants receive exactly the same amount of water.

Step 3:
Check on your plants every three to four days and compare how healthy they look.

Why? How? What?

What do you think will happen to the plant in the cupboard?

How will the plant's leaves change?

(See page 32 for the answer.)

INVESTIGATION 2:

Check Out Transpiration

It's not possible to see the water vapor produced by plants in the air. There is a way, however, to see transpiration in action.

You will need:
- A garden plant with green leaves
- A clear plastic sandwich baggie
- A plastic tie

Step 1:

Choose a leaf on your plant that hangs down rather than stands upright.

Step 2:

Gently position the sandwich baggie over the leaf so that the leaf is completely inside the bag. Secure the bag around the leaf with a plastic tie.

Step 3:

Stand the plant in a sunny spot outside. As photosynthesis occurs, the leaf releases water vapor, which will be trapped inside the plastic bag.

Step 4:

Let the plant stand outside overnight. In the morning, you will see water in the plastic bag. (Ideally you want a leaf that hangs down so the water cannot escape from the bag.) The water vapor released by the leaf has become liquid water. This shows that transpiration took place.

Why? How? What?

What happened to the water vapor overnight to make it change into liquid water?.
(See page 32 for the answer.)

Glossary

atmosphere (AT-muh-sfeer)
The layer of gases surrounding a planet, moon, or star.

carbon dioxide
(KAHR-bun dy-OK-syd)
A clear gas in the air that plants use to make food. When humans and other animals breathe out, they release carbon dioxide into the air.

chlorophyll (KLOR-uh-fil)
The substance that gives plants their green color. Leaves use chlorophyll for making food during photosynthesis.

chloroplasts (KLOR-uh-plasts)
The parts of a plant cell where photosynthesis takes place. Chloroplasts contain chlorophyll.

coniferous (kah-NIH-fur-us)
Referring to trees that often grow in cold, tough habitats and do not lose all their leaves in winter. Many have needlelike leaves.

deciduous (deh-SIH-joo-us)
Referring to trees that drop their leaves in fall or winter to save energy.

global warming
(GLOH-bul WAWRM-ing)
The slow and steady increase in temperatures on Earth caused by gases, including carbon dioxide, that trap the Sun's heat in Earth's atmosphere.

habitats (HA-buh-tats)
Places where animals or plants normally live. A habitat may be a backyard, a forest, the ocean, or a mountainside.

minerals (MIN-rulz)
Solid substances made in nature that are needed by living things for growth and health. Calcium, potassium, copper, and iron are all minerals.

nutrients (NOO-tree-ents)
Substances needed by a plant
or animal to help it live and grow.
Plants take in nutrients from the soil
using their roots.

phloem (FLOW-em)
A system of tubes inside a plant
that carry food from the leaves
through the stems to wherever
it is needed inside the plant.

photosynthesis
(foh-toh-SIN-thuh-sus)
The process by which plants make
food in their leaves using water,
carbon dioxide, and sunlight.

roots (ROOTS) Parts of plants that
usually grow underground and
are used by the plant for taking in
water and nutrients from the soil.

stomata (STOH-mah-tuh)
Microscopic holes on a leaf that
a plant uses for taking in carbon
dioxide and releasing oxygen
and water vapor.

transpiration
(tran-spuh-RAY-shun) The release
of water vapor from a plant's
leaves through evaporation.

water vapor (WAH-ter VAY-pur)
Water that has evaporated and
become a gas floating in the air.

xylem (ZY-lum)
A system of tubes inside a plant
that carry water from the roots,
through the stems, and to the
leaves.

Websites

Due to the changing nature of Internet links,
PowerKids Press has developed an online list
of websites related to the subject of this book.
This site is updated regularly. Please use this
link to access the list:

www.powerkidslinks.com/wop/make/

Read More

Morgan, Sally. *The Plant Cycle*. New York: PowerKids Press, 2009.

Shea, Therese. *Watch Pine Trees Grow*. New York: Gareth Stevens, 2011.

Waldron, Melanie. *Leaves*. Mankato, MN: Capstone Press, 2014.

Index

Answers

INVESTIGATION 1:
The plant in the cupboard will not be as healthy as the other plant as it cannot make food without sunlight. The plant's leaves will eventually lose their green color as they stop producing chlorophyll.

INVESTIGATION 2:
Once it got dark and the temperature cooled outside, the water vapor in the bag cooled, too. The gas condensed and became liquid water.